Movement of The Way

Immersionin Awe, Alignment, and Love

Sheva Ruach

The Sevenfold Way of the Holy Spirit

Chaplain Shawnna Schmidt

Tenuat HaDerekh
Sheva Ruach The Sevenfold Way of the Holy Spirit

Copyright © Chaplain Shawnna Schmidt 2026
Images and text Copyright ©Chaplain Shawnna Schmidt
Editor Aryrejin El
Interior Design S.C. Schmidt
Cover Design S.C Schmidt
Illustrations Copyright © S.C Schmidt
Photographic images used with permission
Shomer Press Publishing
All Rights Reserved
No part of this work may be reproduced without written consent from the Copyright holder.
ISBN paperback 9798988935087

Sheva Ruach

The Sevenfold Way of the Holy Spirit

Tenuat HaDerekh — Movement of the Way
A sacred practice of breath, embodiment, and return
© Chaplain Shawnna Schmidt

If you desire deeper study, Movement of the Way is the foundational text

IMPORTANT NOTICE & PRACTICE DISCLAIMER

Welcome
Tenuat HaDerekh (Movement of The Way) is a gentle, spiritually rooted movement and breath practice inspired by Scripture, embodied prayer, and mindful awareness. This practice is invitational, adaptive, and designed to honor the body as a sacred vessel.

Please Read Before Participating
Tenuat HaDerekh (Movement of The Way) is a spiritual movement and breath practice rooted in Scripture, embodied prayer, and gentle somatic awareness. It is designed to support reflection, grounding, worship, and personal awareness, not to diagnose, treat, or cure any medical or psychological condition.

Personal Responsibility

Assumption of Risk & Release of Liability

By engaging in this practice, you acknowledge and agree that:

You are participating voluntarily

You take responsibility for your own physical, emotional, and spiritual wellbeing

You will seek appropriate professional care when needed

You release the author, editor, instructor, facilitators, and hosts from any liability for injury, loss, or damages, including but not limited to those arising from participation

You agree not to hold any of the above parties responsible for outcomes resulting from your voluntary participation

Spiritual Orientation

This practice is offered from a Messianic faith foundation, rooted in Scripture and the Way of Yeshua (Jesus). Participation does not require theological agreement — only respect for the spiritual framework in which it is presented.

This practice is not a substitute for medical care, physical therapy, mental health treatment, or professional supervision.

No medical or therapeutic claims are made, expressed or implied.

The author, editor, and publishers are not responsible for injuries, discomfort, or adverse effects that may occur during or after participation.

Always consult a qualified healthcare provider before beginning any movement, breath, or wellness practice — especially if you are pregnant, recovering from injury or surgery, living with chronic illness, neurological conditions, heart conditions, or mobility limitations.

Honor Your Body

You are encouraged to:

Move slowly and gently

Modify, adapt, or skip any posture

Rest whenever needed

Stop immediately if anything causes pain, dizziness, distress, or discomfort

Pain is not a spiritual requirement.

Stillness is as valid as movement.

Listening to your body is an act of wisdom.

Adaptive & Inclusive Practice

All postures in Tenuat HaDerekh may be practiced seated, supported, or visualized. There is no "correct" expression — only an honest one.

Choosing rest, stillness, or observation is fully participating.

Final Blessing

May this practice be a place of peace, not pressure.

May it restore, not strain.

May it guide you gently, always toward life.

Table of Content

Movement of the Way, Living Letters
Sheva Ruach Opening Pages
- A Word to the Reader
- How to Use This Immersion

Isaiah 11:2
The Dove Keeps Our Hearts
The Sevenfold Way
Holy Awe / Fear of the Lord
- Letter: Aleph (א)

Reverence / Piety
- Letter: Dalet (ד)

Knowledge / Knowing God Through Relationship
- Letter: Bet (ב)

Courage / Fortitude
- Letter: Gimel (ג)

Counsel / Discernment
 Letter: Vav (ו)

Understanding / Binah
 Letter: Resh (ר)

Wisdom / Holy Fire
 Letter: Shin (ש)

The Seal
- Tav — The Mark of Completion
- Benediction

Inspired Messenger
Other Books By Chaplain Shawnna Schmidt

Seven of the Spirit is a contemplative companion volume within the HaDerekh, The Movement of the Way series.

While Movement of the Way introduces the language, theology, and foundational movements of embodied prayer through the Hebrew letters, Seven of the Spirit offers a focused devotional pathway, inviting practitioners to inhabit the spiritual qualities that shape a life aligned with God's Presence.

This book assumes familiarity with the spirit and posture of HaDerekh, but it may also be used independently by those seeking a gentle, Scripture centered practice rooted in stillness, reverence, and embodied faith.

Together, the HaDerekh series forms a living curriculum:

- Movement of the Way teaches how the body listens
- Seven of the Spirit teaches how the Spirit rests within the body

The Hebrew Letter Movement Poses are based on the Aleph-Bet and form the embodied foundation of this practice.

"What am I looking at?"

Your body belongs in prayer.

Tenuat HaDerekh is an invitation to remember that your body belongs in prayer, that breath is sacred, and that the Way is not hurried but walked — step by step, in presence and trust.

There is nothing to memorize.
You may read, listen, move, or simply rest with the page.
The practice meets you where you are.

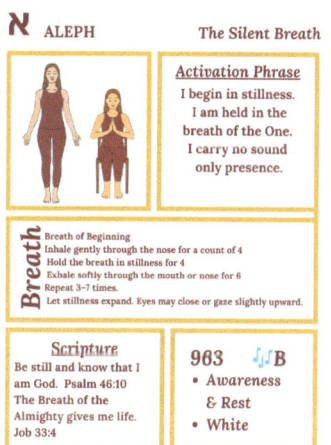

Each posture includes shape, breath, Scripture, and reflection.

If you feel unsure, return to breath.
Breath is always the beginning and the place of return.

Optional tools may be used to round out your prayer time.
These may include simple sounds, timing supports, chromotherapy or other gentle aids that help mark transitions or sustain attention.
Tools do not lead the practice, presence does.

If the posture is not accessible, remain with the breath and intention.

Some letters may appear more than once throughout the book, serving as anchors for beginning, integration, or rest.

HaDerekh
Movement of the Way,
The Living Letters

HaDerekh, The Way is a breath-led, body-based spiritual practice rooted in the Hebrew letters as living forms. It invites readers into embodied prayer through gentle movement, sacred posture, and attentive breath. Not as performance, but as presence.

Drawing from Scripture, Hebrew thought, and the embodied ministry of Yeshua, this book reclaims the body as a sacred vessel, a place where prayer is lived, not merely spoken. Each letter becomes an invitation to listen, align, and move with intention, allowing faith to be carried not only in belief, but in the body itself.

Designed for personal devotion, group practice, and teaching settings, HaDerekh offers adaptive postures, theological reflection, and contemplative guidance accessible to all bodies and abilities.

Silence is honored. Stillness is welcomed. Movement becomes a form of remembering. This book is not meant to be rushed. It is meant to be walked. Because before prayer had words, it had breath. And the body already knows the way.

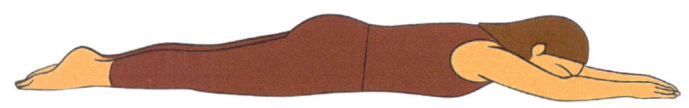

Seven of the Spirit is an embodied prayer journey rooted in Scripture, sacred breath, and the living wisdom of the Hebrew letters. This book invites the reader not merely to reflect on the Sevenfold Spirit of God, but to receive it into the body through stillness, movement, and gentle attentiveness to Presence.

Each section pairs a Hebrew letter with one of the seven spiritual attributes: Awe, Reverence, Knowledge, Courage, Counsel, Understanding, and Wisdom offering a simple posture, breath prayer, blessing, and Scripture for daily or seasonal practice. The movements are quiet, accessible, and non-striving, designed to be practiced alone or within a guided community.

This is not a performance based practice, nor a technique to master. It is a way of dwelling, learning how the body listens, how breath remembers, and how wisdom rests where love is allowed to stay.

The journey concludes with Tav, the closing seal: a Sabbath-shaped completion that gathers what has been received and allows it to rest.

Who This Book Is For

- Individuals seeking a faith centered embodied prayer practice
- Pastors, chaplains, and spiritual directors
- Retreats and small, guided groups with a MOTW leader
- Those longing to move slowly, reverently, and honestly with God

No prior movement experience is required. Only willingness.

Final Note: This book is intended for personal and guided use. For group facilitation or teaching, training in the Movement of the Way framework is recommended.

Where the Dove Rests and the Flames Rise

Sheva Ruach

**The Sevenfold Way of the Holy Spirit
Movement of The Way Immersion
Hebrew Letter Mapping to the Seven Gifts**

The Holy Spirit does not rush the body.
She descends. She rests. She remains.
This seven pose immersion invites you to embody the Seven Gifts of the Holy Spirit through Scripture, gentle prayer, aligned breath, sacred movement, color, and frequency. Each pose builds upon the last, forming a coherent spiral from holy awe to wisdom aflame.

Note To The Reader: If you are new to embodied prayer or desire deeper grounding and stillness practices, Movement of the Way offers foundational teachings such as Sheket (holy stillness) and Eretz (embodied grounding), which beautifully support the practices in this immersion.

Walking with the Dove through the Week
Weekly Flow Option

Sunday: ALEPH | Awe (Holy Stillness)
We begin the week by remembering God is God.
→ Stillness before striving
→ Breath before action

Monday: DALET | Reverence (The Bow)
We approach our responsibilities with humility.
→ Work becomes worship

Tuesday: BET | Knowledge (The Dwelling)
We tend the inner house.
→ Ordering thoughts, habits, and care

Wednesday: GIMEL | Courage (Strength in Motion)
Midweek strength that is heart-led.
→ Love moves us forward

Thursday: VAV | Discernment (Counsel)
We choose wisely as momentum builds.
→ Aligning decisions before the weekend

Friday: AYIN | Understanding (Inner Seeing)
We reflect. We perceive. We soften.
→ Seeing the pattern of the week

Saturday: SHIN | Wisdom (Sabbath Flame)
Fire that burns because the work has stopped.
On Sabbath, we don't seek wisdom, we receive it.

A Note on Sabbath Wisdom

The sequence concludes with Wisdom (Shin) on Saturday / Sabbath. Wisdom is not something we force or chase. It is something we receive in rest. On this day, allow the body to be still longer. Let the flame burn gently. Do not rush to "do" anything with what you receive.

Complete Immersion Practice

The full sequence may also be practiced in one sitting for personal devotion or with a class led by a MOTW leader. When practiced together, the movements form a gentle ascent from holy awe to rested wisdom, mirroring the way the Spirit often teaches: first settling, then aligning, then igniting. Allow extra time for stillness at the end.

A Movement of The Way catechesis without lectures,
theology without argument,
healing without fixing. People feel the truth.

Closing Blessing

The Spirit rests where the body feels safe.
May this practice help you listen more deeply, move more gently, and align more fully with Love.

Isaiah 11:2

The Spirit of the LORD
shall rest upon Him
the Spirit of wisdom and
understanding,
the Spirit of counsel and might,
the Spirit of knowledge
and the fear of the LORD.

The Dove keeps our hearts,
our minds,
and our bodies.

She guards what thinks,
what feels,
and what moves.

She keeps the places where love is learned,
where truth is discerned,
and where rest is finally allowed.

May that keeping be gentle.
May it be complete.
May it be enough.
Shalom.

Invocation Prayer

Holy Spirit,
Breath of God and Giver of Life,
we welcome Your nearness.
Descend upon us gently.
Quiet what is restless.
Awaken what is ready.
Teach our bodies to listen,
our breath to soften,
and our hearts to remain open.
As we move, move within us.
As we rest, rest upon us.
May we receive Your gifts
not by striving,
but by making room.
Amen

Select one opening prayer before beginning the immersion.

Invocation Prayer

Hebrew-inflected

Ruach HaKodesh,
Breath of God, Spirit of the Living One,
we welcome Your nearness.
Descend upon us gently
Ruach Chayyim, breath of life.
Quiet what is restless.
Awaken what is ready.
Teach our bodies to listen
sheket, holy stillness.
Teach our breath to soften
neshimah, sacred breath.
Teach our hearts to remain open
lev niftach, an opened heart.
As we move, move within us.
As we rest, rest upon us.
May we receive Your gifts
not by striving,
but by making room.
Ken yehi ratzon.
May this be Your will.
Amen.

ALEPH

AWE
Holy Stillness

The fear of the LORD is
the beginning of wisdom.
Proverbs 9:10

Breath • Source • Holy Stillness

Fear of the Lord (Awe)

Hebrew Letter: ALEPH (א)

The Spirit of the LORD shall rest upon Him...
Isaiah 11:2

Before movement, there is awe. Before wisdom speaks, the body listens. Aleph is the silent letter. It carries no sound of its own, yet all sound begins within it. It is breath before word, presence before action, God before striving. In Isaiah 11, the Spirit does not rush. It rests. The Fear of the Lord is the first place where the Spirit can settle. Not because the body has achieved something, but because it has become still enough to receive. The Fear of the Lord is not terror. It is holy gravity. The quiet knowing that you are not the center, and that this is good.

In Aleph, the body learns to soften. Muscles release their need to perform. The nervous system settles into safety. The soul remembers it is held. This is where the journey must begin.

Holy Spirit, rest on me.

- Not with effort.
- Not with understanding.
- But with reverence.
- Stillness is not empty.
- It is full of listening.

Here, awe settles the body so wisdom may later rest. Here, breath becomes prayer without words. Here, the Spirit hovers, not demanding, not rushing, but waiting for consent.

> *Be still, and know that I am God. Psalm 46:10*

The beginning of wisdom is not knowing what to do. It is knowing Who is God, and who you are in relation to Him. Aleph teaches the body how to yield without collapse and how to trust without losing self. Let yourself be held here. Nothing is required of you.

> *The fear of the LORD is the beginning of wisdom. Proverbs 9:10*

Closing Reflection
Awe is the doorway through which all wisdom enters. When the body rests in reverence, the Spirit can settle.

God is The Am, who holds me.

Holy Stillness

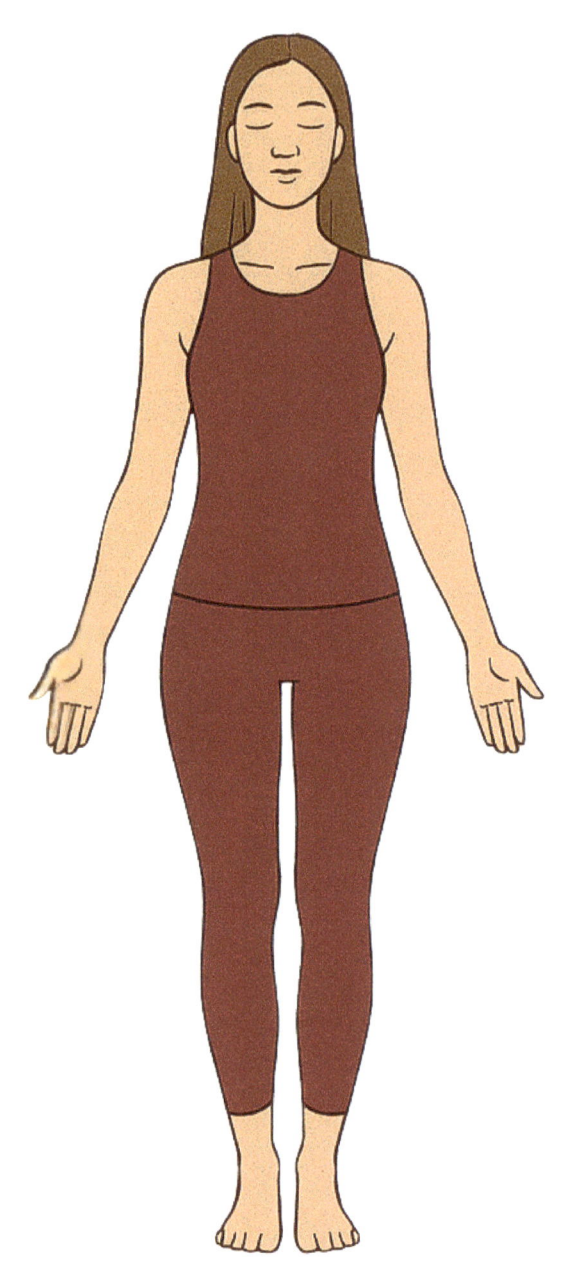

ALEPH *Holy Stillness / Sheket*

Activation Phrase
I rest in holy stillness.
I am held by God.
I do not strive — I listen.

Breath
Breath of Beginning
Inhale gently through the nose for a count of 4
Hold the breath in stillness for 4
Exhale softly through the mouth or nose for 6
Repeat 3–7 times.
Let stillness expand. Eyes may close or gaze slightly upward.

Scripture
Be still and know that I am God.
Psalm 46:10

7.83HZ ♫ C
- Rest / Awareness
- White

Essential Oil: Frankincense

DALET

REVERENCE
The Bow

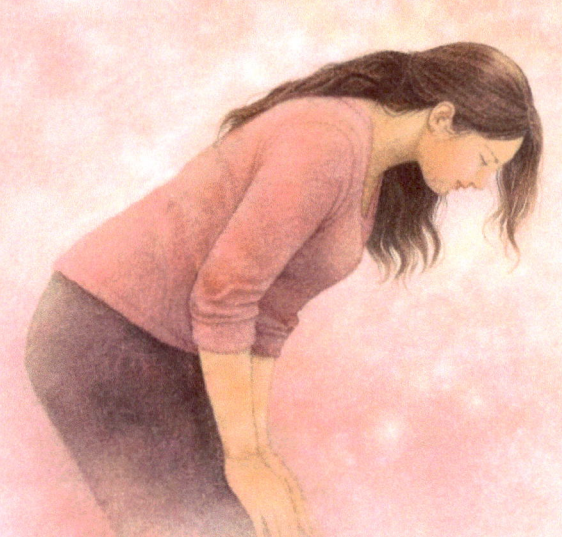

Serve the LORD with fear, and rejoice with trembling. Psalm 2:11

Door • Humility • Holy Receptivity

REVERENCE

Hebrew Letter: DALET (ד)

The Spirit of the LORD shall rest upon Him, the Spirit of wisdom and understanding. Isaiah 11:2

Understanding does not arrive by force. It enters through an open door. Dalet means door, the place where inside meets outside, where what is given must be received. If Aleph taught the body to be still, Dalet teaches the body how to open. Understanding is not analysis. It is not accumulation. It is not mastery. Biblical understanding begins with humility, the willingness to stand at the threshold and admit that wisdom comes from beyond the self. The Spirit of understanding does not push. She waits for the door to be unlatched.

Dalet carries the posture of the poor in spirit, not lacking worth, but lacking pretense. Here, the body softens its defenses. The chest opens without collapsing. The spine learns receptivity without passivity. Understanding settles when striving stops This is why Isaiah names understanding after wisdom, because wisdom must be received, not seized.

Teach my body holy respect.

The body learns to listen without rushing to respond. The mind learns to pause without fear of not knowing. The soul learns that insight is a gift, not a prize.

With humility comes wisdom. Proverbs 11:2

Dalet teaches the body how to stand in the doorway open, attentive, and unguarded without surrendering its integrity. This is holy receptivity. Not empty. Not naive. But willing. Understanding rests where the door is open and the house is prepared.

Open my eyes, that I may behold wondrous things out of Your Torah. Psalm 119:18

Closing Reflection
Understanding does not come by grasping.
It comes by opening.
I do not force the door.
I do not bar it in fear.
I stand ready —
and the Spirit enters.

I approach with honor.

The Sacred Bow

ד DALET — *The Door / Humble Access*

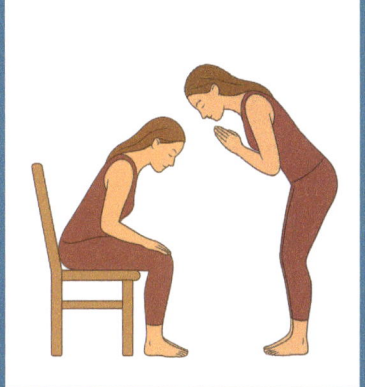

Activation Phrase

I bow in reverence.
Humility opens the door.
I am welcomed in love.

Breath

Inhale (5): Open the heart gently
Pause (2): Stand at the threshold
Exhale (7): Release self-will and soften
- Repeat 3–5 times

Scripture

Come, let us bow down in worship.
Psalm 95:6

174 🎵 D

- *Strength*
- *Soft Rose*

Essential Oil: Myrrh (or Sandalwood)

BET

KNOWLEDGE
The House

By wisdom a house is built...
Proverbs 24:3

House • Belonging • God With Us

KNOWLEDGE

Hebrew Letter: BET (ב)

The Spirit of the LORD shall rest upon Him...
Isaiah 11:2

Before wisdom speaks, before understanding opens, before counsel guides or might strengthens, the Spirit rests. Bet means house. Not a structure of stone, but a place of belonging. A space prepared for presence. A body made ready to host God. The Spirit does not hover endlessly. She rests where she is welcomed. Bet teaches the body how to become a dwelling. Here, faith is no longer an idea. It becomes inhabitable. The shoulders soften. The breath deepens. The inner world steadies.

The body learns:
I am not visited, I am inhabited. This is Emmanuel theology lived in the flesh. God does not rush through the body. He abides. Bet is the courage to let God stay. Not only in moments of prayer, but in movement, in work, in stillness, in breath.

Order my inner house.

*Let them make Me a sanctuary,
that I may dwell among them. Exodus 25:8*

The Spirit rests where striving ceases. Where the house is swept of fear. Where rooms once guarded are opened. Bet is not perfection, it is availability. A home does not need to impress. It needs to receive. This is why Isaiah begins with rest, because wisdom cannot remain where there is no dwelling. The body must become a house before it can carry fire.

Christ in you, the hope of glory. Colossians 1:27

Closing Reflection
I am not empty space. I am a dwelling place. My body is a house for the Spirit of the LORD. Here, you are welcome to rest.

I steward what God entrusts to me.

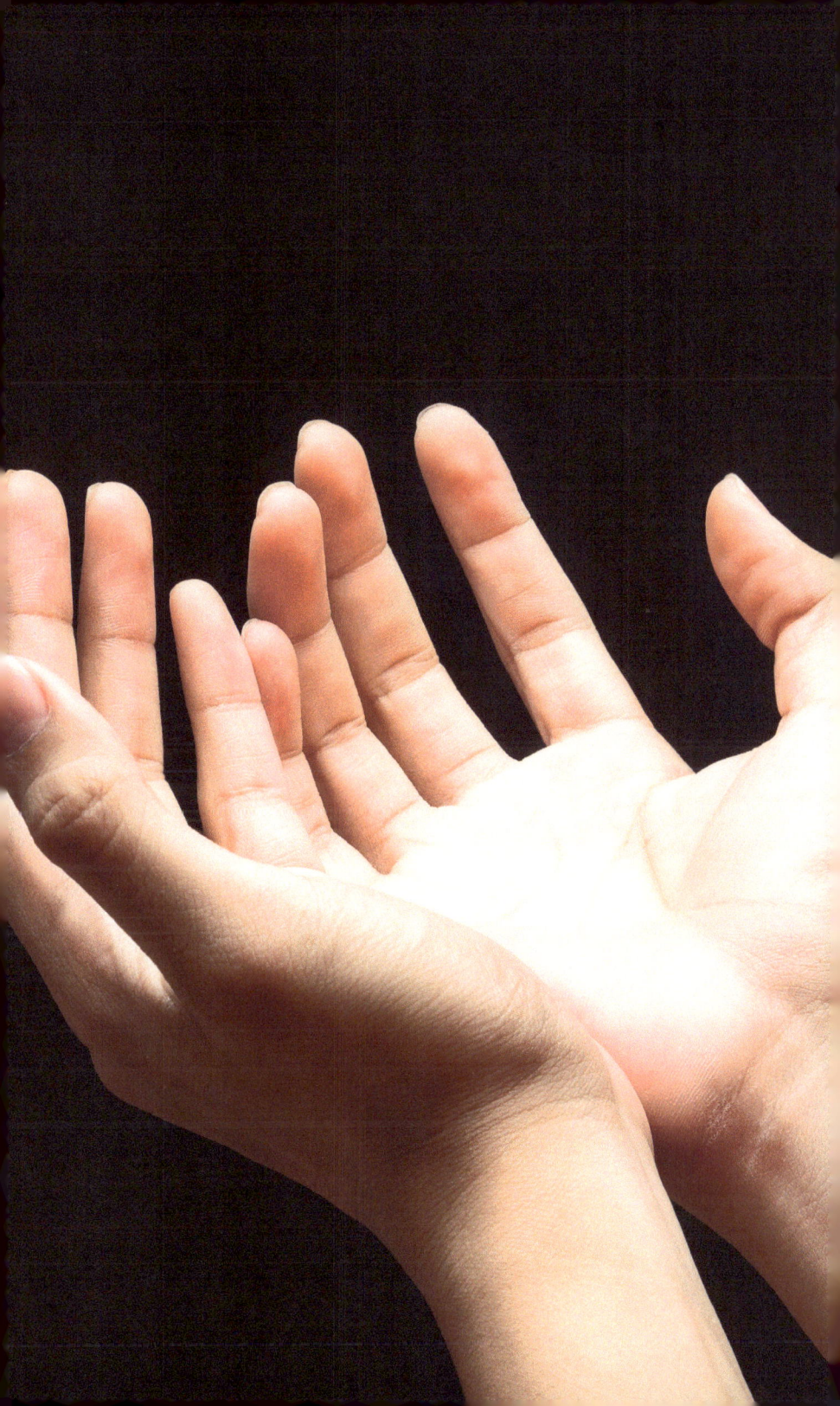

Inner Dwelling

ב

 **BET**   House, Dwelling, Container

Activation Phrase

I am a dwelling place of wisdom.
I carry light with care.
God orders my understanding.

Breath

Inhale (4): Fill the inner house
Hold (3): Gather and contain
Exhale (6): Extend wisely
Repeat 3–5 times

Scripture

Teach us to number our days, that we may gain a heart of wisdom.
Psalm 90:12

285 HZ ♪♪ E

- *Heart*
- *Golden Yellow*

Essential Oil: Cedarwood

GIMEL
COURAGE
The Giving Step

Be strong and courageous...
Joshua 1:9

Giving • Movement
Strength Wrapped in Mercy

Courage In Motion

Hebrew Letter: GIMEL (ג)

The Spirit of the LORD shall rest upon Him. the Spirit of wisdom and understanding, the Spirit of counsel and might... Isaiah 11:2

After the Spirit rests, the body is no longer still. It moves — but not in haste. Gimel is the letter of going forth. It carries the image of one who walks toward another, bearing provision. Not power for domination, but strength for giving. Counsel is not cleverness. Might is not force. In Isaiah, they arrive together because holy strength is guided, and true counsel has weight.

Gimel teaches the body how to move without abandoning presence. Here, courage rises, not from pressure, but from a heart already held. The legs remember how to step forward. The spine carries resolve without rigidity. The arms offer rather than grasp.

Strength wrapped in mercy.

This is strength that knows where it is going because it knows Who goes with it.

> Be strong and courageous...
> for the LORD your God is
> with you wherever you go. Joshua 1:9

Gimel is mercy in motion. It is the willingness to act without needing to control outcomes. It is leadership without striving, authority without violence, obedience without fear. The body learns here that might does not require tension. It requires trust. This is the Spirit's courage, to step forward while remaining rooted in God.

> The LORD is my strength and my shield. Psalm 28:7

Gimel comes after Bet because action must flow from dwelling. Otherwise, movement becomes anxiety and strength becomes performance. But when the Spirit rests first, movement becomes ministry.

Closing Reflection
I move forward with God, not ahead of Him.
Strength flows through mercy.
Courage rises from presence.
The Spirit of counsel and might walks with me.

I move forward with love.

Strength in Motion

ג GIMEL

Strength in Motion
Giving Flow

Activation Phrase

I move forward in love.
Strength flows through mercy.
Courage rises from presence.

Breath

Inhale (5): Expand the heart
Exhale (5): Step forward gently
Optional whisper: "Gimel... love moves me."
Repeat 3–5 cycles

Scripture

Be strong and courageous... for the Lord your God is with you. Joshua 1:9

528 HZ ♪♪F

- *Heart*
- *Emerald Green*

Essential Oil: Bergamot

VAV

COUNSEL

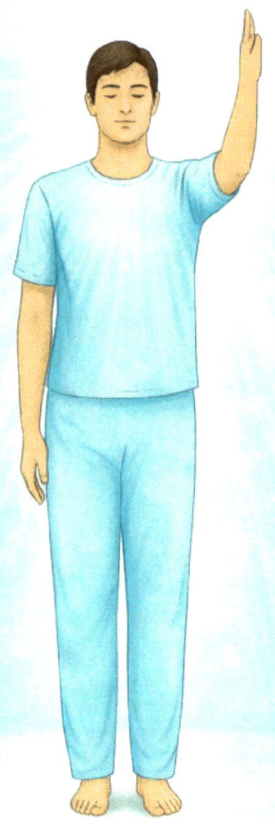

"I will counsel you with
My loving eye upon you."

- Psalm 32:8

Connector • Alignment • The Holy Turn

COUNSEL

Hebrew Letter: VAV (ו)

> The Spirit of the LORD shall rest upon Him the Spirit of wisdom and understanding, the Spirit of counsel and might... Isaiah 11:2

Vav means *and.* It is the smallest letter, yet it holds things together. Vav is the holy hinge, the place where movement pauses and direction is chosen. If Gimel taught the body how to step forward, Vav teaches the body when to turn. Counsel is not impulse. It is not reaction. It is not hesitation. Counsel is alignment. Here, the Spirit trains the body to listen mid-motion to sense when to continue, when to wait, when to redirect, and when to stop.

The shoulders soften. The neck releases its urgency. The head learns to turn without fear. This is discernment that does not rush speech and judgment that does not harden the heart.

> *I will instruct you and teach you in the way you should go; I will counsel you with My eye upon you. Psalm 32:8*

Vav joins wisdom to action and understanding to courage. Without counsel, strength becomes reckless. Without counsel, movement fractures. But with the Spirit's counsel, every step remains connected to God. Vav is obedience that listens while moving. The body learns here that discernment is not paralysis. It is responsiveness.

*In all your ways acknowledge Him,
and He will make your paths straight. Proverbs 3:6*

Vav comes after courage because discernment requires bravery, the courage to change course when pride wants to continue. This is the Spirit teaching the body how to remain aligned even when the way bends.

Closing Reflection
I am not driven, I am guided.
I pause, I listen, I turn as You lead.
The Spirit of counsel keeps me aligned with God.

*Bridge heaven and earth through me.
I choose in alignment.*

The Bridge

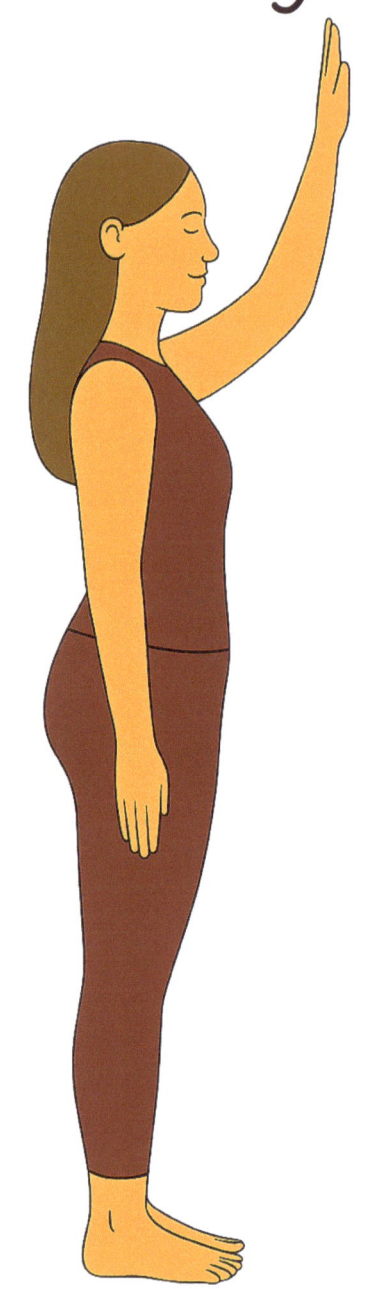

VAV

The Bridge Between

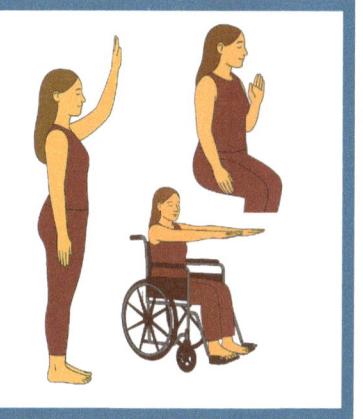

Activation Phrase

I am aligned.
I choose wisely.
Heaven and earth meet through me.

Breath
Inhale (5): Draw breath from earth to crown
Hold (2): Stand in the center
Exhale (5): Release from crown to earth
Visualize a column of light through the spine
Repeat 3–5 times

Scripture
I will instruct you and teach you in the way you should go.
Psalm 32:8

741 ♪♪G
- Breath
- Teal

Essential Oil: Frankincense

AYIN

UNDERSTANDING

Inner Seeing

"Then he opened their eyes
and their sight was restored..."

Mark 8:25

Eye • Insight • Seeing as God Sees

UNDERSTANDING

Hebrew Letter: AYIN (ע)

The Spirit of the LORD shall rest upon Him the Spirit of wisdom and understanding... Isaiah 11:2

Understanding is not effort. It is sight restored. Ayin means eye, not the eye that scans for threat, but the eye that learns how to see again. If Vav taught the body how to align, Ayin teaches the body how to perceive. Understanding does not rush to conclusions. It lingers. It listens with the eyes open. Here, the Spirit widens vision, beyond appearances, beyond assumptions, beyond fear.

The face softens.
The brow releases.
The nervous system lets go of vigilance.
The body discovers that it does not need to strain to see clearly. Clarity arrives when fear loosens its grip.

Then He opened their minds to understand the Scriptures. Luke 24:45

Clarity without fear.

Understanding is opened. It is not seized. This is why Isaiah pairs wisdom with understanding, because wisdom without perception becomes rigid, and perception without wisdom becomes unstable. Ayin holds them together. The Spirit of understanding trains the body to recognize truth without panic, to see patterns without judgment, to discern God's hand without control.

> *Open my eyes, that I may behold wondrous things from Your Torah. Psalm 119:18*

Ayin teaches the body to see from rest. Not every truth must be explained. Not every mystery must be resolved. Some things are understood only when the eyes rest and the heart is unafraid.

Closing Reflection
I see without striving.
I perceive without fear.
The Spirit of understanding opens my eyes
 to what God is already doing.

I see as God sees.

The Open Eye

 **AYIN** — *To See Beyond Seeing*

Activation Phrase
I see as God sees.
I perceive without fear.
Understanding settles within me.

Breath
Inhale (4): Receive clarity
Exhale (6): Soften the eyes and mind
Optional: eyes gently closed or unfocused
Repeat 3–5 times

Scripture
Open my eyes, that I may behold wondrous things out of Your Torah. Psalm 119:18

825 HZ ♪♪ A
- Heart
- Green

Essential Oil: Blue Tansey / Frankincense

SHIN

Holy Fire

*"If any of you lacks wisdom,
let him ask God."*

James 1:5

Fire • Presence • Indwelling Light

WISDOM

Hebrew Letter: SHIN (ש)

The Spirit of the LORD shall rest upon Him, the Spirit of wisdom and understanding... Isaiah 11:2

Wisdom does not arrive first. She comes last. Not because she is distant, but because she requires readiness. Shin is fire, not the fire that consumes, but the fire that abides. If understanding taught the eyes how to see, Shin teaches the whole body how to hold what it sees. Wisdom is not information. It is union. It is truth that has passed through awe, dwelling, movement, alignment, and perception and has not fractured the soul. This is why Isaiah names wisdom alongside understanding not as an achievement, but as a resting presence. The fire of Shin does not scorch the nervous system. It warms it. The crown lifts without strain. The spine lengthens without effort. The breath rises gently. The body becomes trustworthy enough for fire.

For the LORD gives wisdom; from His mouth come knowledge and understanding. Proverbs 2:6

Let me burn with love, never consumed

Shin carries three flames, often understood as breath, fire, and Spirit, not separate, but one presence moving in fullness. Here, Wisdom is no longer sought. She is received. The Spirit does not shout instructions. She illumines the path already beneath your feet.

> *Your word is a lamp to my feet and a light to my path. Psalm 119:105*

Wisdom rests where striving has ended. Not because the journey is over but because the body has learned how to walk with God. This is holy fire that stays.

Closing Reflection
I do not grasp for Wisdom.
I receive her.
The fire of God rests within me
not to consume,
but to illumine.
The Spirit of wisdom abides.

I burn with love and am not consumed.

The Flame of Presence

 **SHIN**

Flame of Revelation
Flame of Divine Presence

Activation Phrase

Holy fire dwells within me.
I burn with wisdom, not consumption.
The Spirit rests upon me.
I am illumined, not overwhelmed.

Breath

Inhale (6):
Draw breath up through the spine to the crown,
imagining a gentle flame kindling above the head.
Exhale (6):
Let the flame soften and spread downward through the heart,
warming but not forcing.
Optional whisper on exhale:
"Shin... Holy fire, rest upon me."
Repeat 3–5 cycles, then pause in awareness..

Scripture
"The Spirit of the Lord shall rest upon Him." Isaiah 11:2

963 HZ ♪♪ B
- Rest / Awareness
- White

Essential Oils:
Frankincense

TAV

SEAL OF COMPLETION

*"I am sealed in truth.
I am whole in You."*

*I am the Aleph and the Tav,
the Beginning and the End."
Revelation 22:13*

Mark • Completion • Faithfulness in Rest

SEAL

Hebrew Letter: TAV (ת)

The Spirit of the LORD shall rest upon Him...
Isaiah 11:2

Tav is the last letter. Not because nothing follows but because what was given has now been received. Tav means mark. A sign of covenant. A seal of belonging. A completion that does not rush forward. If Aleph taught the body how to be still in awe, Tav teaches the body how to remain faithful in rest. This is where the Spirit no longer hovers. She abides. Isaiah begins with rest and Tav returns us there, transformed. The journey has shaped the body. Awe has steadied it. Dwelling has housed it. Movement has strengthened it. Counsel has aligned it. Understanding has clarified it. Wisdom has warmed it. Now, the Spirit seals what has been formed. Tav is obedience that no longer strains. Faithfulness that does not perform. Presence that does not seek permission. The body bears the mark of what it has walked through.

This is not a mark of fear. It is a mark of belonging. The Spirit rests because the house is trustworthy now. The fire remains because the vessel can carry it. Here, the nervous system settles into assurance. The breath finds its natural rhythm. The soul rests without drifting. Nothing more needs to be added.

It is finished. John 19:30

Tav does not end the Way. It confirms it.
You do not leave this place, you carry it forward.

Closing Reflection
I am sealed in God's presence.
 What has been formed in me remains.
The Spirit of the LORD rests
 and so do I.

I am sealed in truth.
I am whole in You.

The Gifts of the Spirit are not received all at once, they are walked into the body, from awe to union, from earth to heaven.

Seal of Completion

ת

 **TAV** — *Mark of Completion*

Activation Phrase
I rest in completion.
I am sealed in truth. Wisdom abides in me.

Breath
Inhale (5): Receive wholeness
Exhale (7): Rest in completion
Let breath become natural after 3 cycles

Scripture
I am the Aleph and the Tav, the Beginning and the End. Revelation 22:13

432 ♪♪B
- Whole body Integration
- Golden White / Violet

Essential Oil: Frankincense or Cedarwood

Benediction

May the Spirit who descended
now remain.
May wisdom rest in your stillness,
understanding soften your seeing,
and discernment guide your steps.
May courage rise without force,
knowledge dwell without burden,
and reverence keep you near.
May the fire of God burn gently
within you, a light that warms,
a flame that does not consume.
Go in peace.
The Spirit rests with you.

Select one closing prayer.

Hebrew-inflected Benediction

Ruach Shokhenet, the Spirit who dwells.
May wisdom rest in Your stillness
chochmah received, not pursued.
May understanding soften your seeing
binah opening gently.
May discernment guide your steps
etzah given in love.
May courage rise without force
gevurah held with compassion.
May knowledge dwell without burden
da'at rooted in truth.
May reverence keep you near
yirah as holy awe.
May the fire of God burn gently within you
esh kodesh, holy flame
a light that warms,
a fire that does not consume.
Go in peace
lech b'shalom.
The Spirit rests with you.
Ruach Adonai shochelet alecha.

Seven flames.

One Spirit.

One Way.

Inspired Messenger

Chaplain Shawnna Schmidt

Chaplain Shawnna Schmidt is a faith-rooted teacher, chaplain, and embodied-prayer guide whose work bridges Scripture, breath, and the living wisdom of the body. She is the founder of Movement of the Way (Tenuat HaDerekh)—a sacred movement practice rooted in the Hebrew Scriptures, the Messianic path of Yeshua, and the ancient understanding that faith is something we walk, not merely believe.

Drawing from Hebraic thought, embodied worship, nervous-system awareness, and a lifetime of pastoral care, Shawnna teaches that the body is not separate from prayer, it is the vessel through which prayer becomes lived. Her work gently restores connection between Body, Soul, and Spirit through movement, breath, Scripture, and stillness.

Shaped by motherhood, caregiving, resilience, and wonder, her calling has been refined through both joy and trial. She writes and teaches for those who love God deeply yet long to feel grounded, safe, and at home in their bodies again.

Each book in the HaDerekh series is offered not as instruction alone, but as invitation, an unfolding walk back to the ancient path, where the Word becomes flesh once more, and the body remembers how to say yes.

Books
By Chaplain Shawnna Schmidt

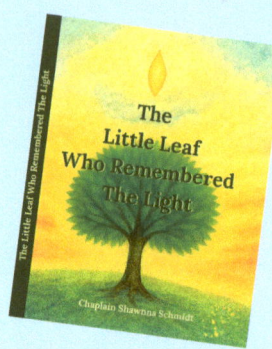

The Little Leaf Who Remembered The Light

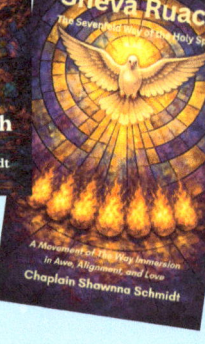

Movement of The Way Devotionals

Shomer Press

Devotional Series

Align With Love

- **Awaken** – A gentle stirring of the heart — inviting women to rise from spiritual slumber and rediscover the nearness of God's presence.
- **Arise** – A call to step forward with courage, truth, and purpose, standing firmly in the identity Heaven has spoken over you.
- **Abide** – A devotional of rest and rootedness — learning to dwell in God's love, peace, and steadying rhythm of grace.
- **Anointed** – A blessing-filled journey that reminds women of the oil, favor, and divine purpose poured over their lives since the beginning.

Series Summary:

A four-part devotional path offering 53 weeks of inspiration, Scripture, healing reflection, and alignment with Love.

Be, A Story of Orgin

A contemplative journey back to the beginning — where Light, Breath, and the Creator's Voice shaped all things. A poetic exploration of who we are, where we come from, and the divine resonance written into every soul.

Heart of Gratitude
52-Week Journal

A year of cultivating beauty, awareness, and thankfulness — where creativity and reflection open the heart to joy, hope, and deeper connection with God.

HaShem
Healing Through The Names of God

A sacred encounter with the Holy One through His revealed Names — exploring their frequencies, meanings, and the healing they release into body, soul, and spirit.

COMING SOON

Frequency Doula

A contemplative journey back to the beginning — where Light, Breath, and the Creator's Voice shaped all things. A poetic exploration of who we are, where we come from, and the divine resonance written into every soul.

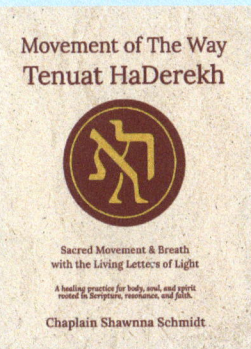

Movement of the Way

Where movement meets prayer, and awareness becomes worship.
Movement of the Way invites you into a rhythm of embodied faith — cultivating gratitude, presence, and spiritual alignment through weekly reflections and soul-tending practices. connection with God.

First Light

More than a study, First Light is a remembrance a return to the sacred truth that we were formed in Light, made to carry Light, and forever guided by the Light that spoke the world into being.
A timeless resource for seekers, teachers, and anyone longing to understand the radiance at the beginning of every story and the Light that still leads us on.

www.ingramcontent.com/pod-product-compliance
Lightning Source LLC
Chambersburg PA
CBHW042305150426
43197CB00001B/23